10/09 Quest

Tornadoes

By Jim Mezzanotte

Science and curriculum consultant: Debra Voege, M.A.,
science and math curriculum resource teacher

Reading specialist: Linda Cornwell, Literacy Connections Consulting

WEEKLY READER®
PUBLISHING

Please visit our web site at **www.garethstevens.com**.
For a free color catalog describing our list of high-quality books,
call 1-800-542-2595 (USA) or 1-800-387-3178 (Canada).
Our fax: (877) 542-2596

Library of Congress Cataloging-in-Publication Data

Mezzanotte, Jim.
    Tornadoes / by Jim Mezzanotte ; science and curriculum consultant, Debra Voege.
      p. cm. — (Wild weather)
    Includes bibliographical references and index.
    ISBN-10: 1-4339-2351-3   ISBN-13: 978-1-4339-2351-7 (lib. bdg.)
    ISBN-10: 1-4339-2365-3   ISBN-13: 978-1-4339-2365-4 (pbk.)
    1. Tornadoes—Juvenile literature. I. Title.
QC955.2.M493   2010
551.55'3—dc22   2009001946

This edition first published in 2010 by
Weekly Reader® Books
An Imprint of Gareth Stevens Publishing
1 Reader's Digest Road
Pleasantville, NY 10570-7000 USA

Copyright © 2010 by Gareth Stevens, Inc.

Executive Managing Editor: Lisa M. Herrington
Senior Editor: Barbara Bakowski
Creative Director: Lisa Donovan
Designer: Melissa Welch, *Studio Montage*
Photo Researcher: Diane Laska-Swanke

Photo credits: Cover, title © Tim Samaras/Weatherpix Stock Images; pp. 3, 4, 8, 14, 18, 22, 24
© PhotoDisc/Extraordinary Clouds; pp. 5, 6, 9, 12 © Weatherpix Stock Images; pp. 7, 10 Scott M.
Krall/© Gareth Stevens, Inc.; p. 11 © Eric Nguyen/Jim Reed Photography/Photo Researchers, Inc.;
p. 13 © Joseph Golden/Photo Researchers, Inc.; p. 15 NOAA; p. 16 Jocelyn Augustino/FEMA; p. 17
© AP Images; p. 19 © Howard Bluestein/Photo Researchers, Inc.; p. 20 © Eric Nguyen/Jim Reed
Photography/CORBIS; p. 21 © Tom Bean/CORBIS

Printed in the United States of America

1 2 3 4 5 6 7 8 9 10 12 11 10 09

Table of Contents

Words in **boldface** are defined in the glossary.

CHAPTER 1
Here Comes a Twister!

The sky is dark with storm clouds.
You hear a roaring sound.
A tube-shaped cloud stretches to the ground. It is a **tornado!**

The sky grows dark as a tornado hits.

A tornado is a strong wind that spins in a circle. It is also called a twister. It can move across the ground as fast as a car.

Tornadoes are loud! The spinning winds sound like a jet plane, a rocket, or a train.

This tornado spins toward a farm in South Dakota.

The United States gets about a thousand tornadoes each year. Tornadoes often hit an area in the center of the country. It is called **Tornado Alley.**

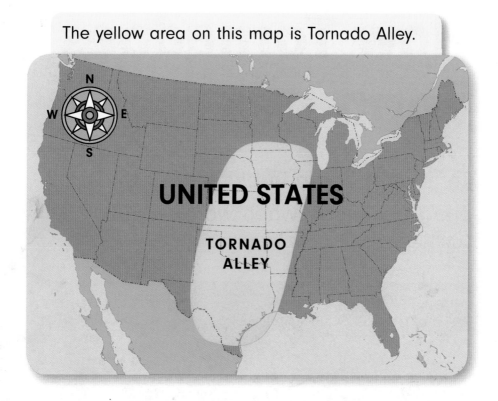

The yellow area on this map is Tornado Alley.

UNITED STATES

TORNADO ALLEY

CHAPTER 2
How Tornadoes Form

Tornadoes begin in big storm clouds.
The clouds form when warm, wet
air rises.

Most storm clouds are wider at the top than at the bottom.

High in the sky, the wet air cools. Drops of water join together and form clouds. The drops get heavier and fall as rain.

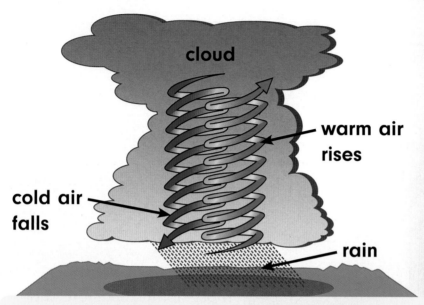

cloud

warm air
rises

cold air
falls

rain

Inside a cloud, warm air rises and cold air falls.
A tube of spinning air forms.

The rain pulls down cold air.
The cold air meets the rising
warm air. The warm air and
cold air twist around.

Part of the cloud grows downward. A tube of spinning air reaches toward the ground. It is shaped like a **funnel.**

A funnel cloud forms during a storm in Kansas.

When the funnel touches the ground, a tornado is born. Strong winds suck up dirt, trees, and even houses!

Waterspouts are not as wide as tornadoes on land.

Sometimes, a funnel moves across a lake or sea. It becomes a **waterspout.** Water is sucked into the funnel.

CHAPTER 3
Deadly Tornadoes

Tornadoes cause damage in some places. They can flatten houses and other buildings.

The deadliest tornado ever to hit the United States was in 1925. It wiped out whole towns. Almost 700 people died.

In 1925, a killer tornado sped through Missouri, Illinois, and Indiana. It left many places in ruins.

Tornadoes pick up objects and throw them into the air. This car landed upside down in a field.

A tornado can toss animals, people, and cars into the air. A waterspout may suck fish from water and drop them onto land!

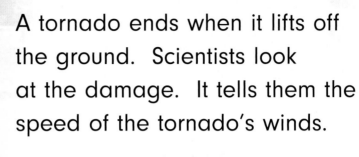

A tornado ends when it lifts off the ground. Scientists look at the damage. It tells them the speed of the tornado's winds.

A tornado blew roofs off some homes on this street. Other houses were not harmed.

CHAPTER 4
Tornado Safety

Scientists watch for tornadoes. They use special tools to track storms. They look at pictures taken from space, too.

Scientists track a tornado crossing an open field.

When a tornado is coming, radio and TV stations warn people. In some places, **sirens** sound.

How do people stay safe from a tornado? They go indoors and keep away from windows. Some people go to underground rooms called storm cellars.

Tornadoes are scary! You can plan ahead. Listen for warnings and know how to stay safe.

A storm cellar is a safe place to go when a tornado is coming.

Glossary

funnel: a tube that has a wide top and a narrow bottom. A tornado is shaped like a funnel.

sirens: machines used to sound warnings

tornado: a tube of spinning air that stretches from a storm cloud to the ground

Tornado Alley: an area in the central United States where tornadoes happen most often

waterspout: a tube of swirling wind and water. It forms when a tornado passes over a lake or sea.

For More Information

Books

Tornadoes. What on Earth? (series). David and Helen
   Orme (Scholastic Library Publishing, 2005)

Wind. Weather Around You (series). Anita Ganeri
   (Gareth Stevens Publishing, 2005)

Web Sites

FEMA for Kids: Tornadoes
www.fema.gov/kids/tornado.htm
Read kids' stories about tornadoes. Take a quiz and
watch a video, too.

Weather Wiz Kids: Tornadoes
www.weatherwizkids.com/tornado.htm
Make a tornado in a bottle or a jar!

Publisher's note to educators and parents: Our editors have carefully reviewed these
web sites to ensure that they are suitable for children. Many web sites change frequently,
however, and we cannot guarantee that a site's future contents will continue to meet our
high standards of quality and educational value. Be advised that children should be closely
supervised whenever they access the Internet.

Index

About the Author

Jim Mezzanotte has written many books for children. He lives in Milwaukee, Wisconsin, with his wife and two sons. He has always been interested in weather, especially big storms.